This book is about growing up with what one is given, what one is born into. It is about the complexity and mystery of coming of age, the dance between delight and disappointment, terror and awe, right and wrong as one emerges into personhood and consciousness and thus the loss of innocence. It is about the formation of self, what one picks up, how one is affected and shaped by culture and the context of birth order, parents and siblings, extended family, community and landscape. Growing up on the prairie without amenities, on the edge of civilization, always aware of the boreal forest a little further North, has coloured the way I see things, what I bring into the world through my work, the way I am. With the whole of me, through telling, I have embraced two centuries.

details from the edge of the village

Pierrette Requier

Frontenac House
Calgary, Alberta

Copyright © 2009 by Pierrette Requier

All rights reserved, including moral rights. No part of this publication may be reproduced or transmitted in any form or by any means electronic or mechanical including recording, photocopying, or any information storage retrieval system without permission in writing from the author or publisher or ACCESS copyright, except by a reviewer or academic who may quote brief passages in a review or critical study.

Book and cover design: Epix Design
Cover Image: Ian Sheldon
Author photo: Fred Katz, Katz Studio, Edmonton

Library and Archives Canada Cataloguing in Publication
Requier, Pierrette
    Details from the edge of the village / Pierrette Requier.
Poems.
Text mostly in English with some in French.
ISBN 978-1-897181-24-9

    I. Title.
PS8635.E68D48 2009   C811'.6   C2009-900147-0

We acknowledge the support of the Canada Council for the Arts for our publishing program. We also acknowledge the support of The Alberta Foundation for the Arts.

 Canada Council for the Arts   Conseil des Arts du Canada   

Printed and bound in Canada
Published by Frontenac House Ltd.
1138 Frontenac Avenue S.W.
Calgary, Alberta, T2T 1B6, Canada
Tel: 403-245-2491 Fax: 403-245-2380
editor@frontenachouse.com   www.frontenachouse.com

Second printing October 2009

To my son Christian and his wife Marie France, and Marianne.

To my mom Roseanne and my dad Edouard.

To my settler grandparents, *mes mémères* and *mes pépères,* and my great grandparents.

To my siblings: Roland, Denise, Suzanne, Jacques, Gilles, Guy, Charles, Michel, Marilyne, Richard, their spouses, their children, and grandchildren.

To precious Hayley, who comes to the readings.

To my four other sisters: Louise Décosse, Brenda Love, Eloise Petrin, and Anna Radyo.

To the Earth community that sustains and holds us all.

my fictions

These prose poems are not straight facts but composites, concocted with details both real and invented, and are therefore my fictions. In this book I tell tall tales, *je raconte des histoires*, about growing up in the fifties and sixties, the fourth of eleven in a family of French origin in a Northern Alberta village. Any one of my siblings, I suspect, would tell the stories differently, would add other details, provide a different point of view, spin his or her own sets of tales.

note about the vernacular

Some of the French words have been spelled phonetically to do justice to the local flavour of Northern Alberta French with which I grew up. I take full responsibility for using some commonly used words that would be considered incorrect in more formal written texts.

contents

jack rabbit 13
pictures 15
how i came 16
ghosts 17
waves 18
mes pépères 19
Mom's *Maman* 20
disappears 21
la survivante 22
balloon 23
violon 24
Mom's rituals 25
mother-in-law 26
le déluge 27
telling 28
Père Noël 29
mon beau sapin 30
au feu 31
patinoire 32
free skating 33
la cabane 34
honey 36
champ de patates 37
running water 39
le bain du samedi soir 40
la fille 41
school 42
common sense 43
les mystères du tiroir à Dad 44
infection 45
blue 46
boîte à bois 47
amenities 48
operator 49
the other side of rain 50
customers 51
beauties 52
exactly right 53
le rigodon du pain béni 54

four squares and "Hey, you!"........................56
Nom de Dieu!....................................58
portrait de noces................................59
toots..60
falling from grace................................61
stopped short....................................62
cavities...63
baby sitting 64
ma marraine....................................65
des belles noces 66
ordination 67
small white coffins..............................68
marionnettiste.................................69
accordéon......................................70
grand raconteur................................71
first kiss 72
swimming lessons.................................73
relax..74
truck stop.......................................75
clean up duties..................................76
summer of '66....................................77
Ca-na-da! and burn your bra!.....................78
spark plugs for God's sake 79
élévateurs.....................................80
two uncle Als....................................81
ma tante Eva's ways............................82
the ascension of *ma tante Bartine*..............83
impact...84
Mom's funny ideas................................85
found poem 1.....................................86
found poem 2 God is my helmet...................87
Notre Père.....................................88
Our Father.......................................89
buns...90
found poem 3 fifty-three........................91
diagnosis 92
getting it.......................................93
Halloween Day 1999...............................94
trouble..95

placing Mom 96
Thursdays with Mom 97
sewing basket 98
the boyfriend 99
double bed. 100
c'est dur 101
dépouillement. 102
moving Mom 103
panic 104
Greyhound Bus north 105
Afterword. 106
Acknowledgements 108

details
from
the edge
of the
village

jack rabbit

I didn't know why they called some men Toms and some Johns.

It all started with a scary feeling I got in the dark sometimes. When I was in bed late at night and couldn't sleep. Mom, alone with the eight of us, Dad was away *au chantier*, had called my older brother in "that voice" which spelled alarm and made me hold my breath. The feeling of alarm was mixed with something else. Sex. Not that I was supposed to know the word or what it meant. But I'd overheard the big kids talking about the rape of a girl in a hotel room in the next town and when I told Mom she had only gotten very angry, a dark-eyed, closed-door, we-don't-ever-pronounce-or-think-these-words-in-this-house kind of anger. And I went back to pretending I didn't know and that there was no "danger", but there it was.

Hearing my older sisters get up and talk in muffled voices, and waiting until there were more spaces between their words, I knew it was okay for me to get up too; become part of this mysterious late night meeting. After all, I was next in line and sometimes considered one of the big kids. I did come before that whole row of little boys all in deep sleep by now. Downstairs, the older-brother-become-the-man-of-the-house kept checking the lock on the front room door that was always kept locked anyway. He kept throwing furtive glances out the window. Then at Mom.

Still nervous, pacing, and holding her arms like half-folded wings, Mom said more than she normally would. She had undressed to go to bed and as usual had folded her clothes as she always did and put them on the chair beside her bed so she could dress quickly in the morning. Then slipping into her nightgown she noticed that it was full moon and had decided to look at the sky before going to bed. She liked to look out into the starry skies, to check the weather, to think of Dad away, in his bunk. Parting the sheers, she came face to face with a man. Nose pressed against the window, hands cupping his eyes, he was intent on seeing. Startled, she froze. He turned, and hopped away like a frightened jack rabbit.

Quickly, quietly she drew the curtains. Held her heart. Was it the village priest or the town idiot? she wondered. She couldn't bear to think of it! One would be a kind of sacrilege, the other a brush with insanity. She really didn't know, she said. Either way, it was bad. And she didn't want to let bad in. We were safe. Even though there was still no streetlight on our corner at the edge of the village where we lived.

pictures

i remember things from before i was born from Mom's stories and by looking in the eyes of the people in the pictures in Mom's photo albums   how *Mémère* always looked worried   how on my Mom and Dad's wedding day their neighbour read their tea cups   said they would never be rich but would always have enough   how Mom and Dad's love was as huge and clear as the Peavine Creek sky was blue with only one small cloud in it   like a small lamb in that whole immense mystery   how Mom and Dad looked into each other's eyes the morning after their wedding and cried   both of them cried   how my Dad said you are so young   how my Mom had decided not to wait for the other younger man who had gone to war   who never returned   how my Mom asked my Dad out for the first date   how they were married a few months after that and had their first child a son a few months after that   that's how it all started   and

how i came

one late September night i finally decided just to slip from Mom's womb   that's how i was born   because that afternoon Mom had laboured too much to be in labour   she'd finished digging *tout le grand champ de patates*   had bagged our supply for winter   i was thin-skinned and skinny so skinny i was nicknamed *manche à balai* and i had this dread of *rester* stuck   we lived in gumbo country and in rainy weather the rutted roads became *impassable*   and before moving to that house on the edge of the village   where there were no sidewalks and not even a streetlamp   we'd had to live on the farm again for spring and summer and part of fall because after the seventh child we'd outgrown our tiny house on the other side of the tracks   and when it rained for three days i saw fear build in Mom's eyes when she looked out the window   when Dad wasn't coming back home with *les commissions* Mom just knew he'd stopped at the bar again and she'd busy herself   try to hold it all together   and she just didn't know how long he would be and what she'd do if she ran out of formula for the baby or if one of *ses p'tits* got sick with a high fever   and that's when worry hung in the air   like static electricity

ghosts

when my throat was scratchy and my head throbbed and my nose burned from dry cold   when i didn't want to get out of bed the ghosts of my settler ancestors came for me lost   adrift   awailing   rattling old dry bones   and i get that they want me to speak for them   and my first thought is there is nothing to say   there are no words for their less-than-modest beginnings   for the morsels of story that fell through the cracks   for the crumbs of anecdotes that left a sketchy path   what is the word for their beginning again and again   for an unsettling settling we have been taught to forget   and i sit in *la prairie à en p'us finir* where they sweated and toiled   I fumble in my head   poke   find   "bleak" and   "sparse"   see "slough" and "creek" and a row of skimpy trees as i spit out mouthfuls of mosquitoes   see their cattle die of swamp fever and one of their two horses step on its own tongue while grazing and pull it right out   as i see two sets of great-grandparents die in their shacks

waves

chill wind
restless
with *revenants*
burial hasn't
kept the ghosts
under
or put
them all
to rest
at least not
the great grandfather
the one
without
a headstone
who floats up
who waves and
waves jerkily
crazed
with fear
white as a sheet
seems his tongue
got cut out too
this ghost
looks as if
he's been
at sea
softens as
i foolishly
wave back
let him know
i know
he was here

mes pépères

both came West on trains   ferried across bodies of water finally reaching destinations by wagon   both broke land one was hard the other soft   one sat with a ramrod straight back smiled restrainedly when he'd had a little cognac and told his one joke   his whole life he had only one joke and it was his brother Jess's joke   the one about *le gars qui était assez paresseux qui voulait même pas se lever de sa chaise une fois par mois pour changer la page du calendrier*   after many hard years the soft one stands lank stooped and aged   i like to imagine him still young and smiling as he carries my father his firstborn on his shoulders   as he later pulls the only two grandchildren he will ever know in a wooden wagon he'd fabricated offering them surplus eggs to throw against *les graineries*   one had a *régime* and in his house no one worked past nine o'clock at night   it was early to bed and early to rise   the other had all the time in the world   was said by *certaines dames des alentours* to be *un vrai gentleman qui pouvait don' pas handler les gens de travers   qui voyait pas la différence entre les Français les Anglais les Ukrainiens les Allemands les Polonais les Indiens   ici   dans le New World   dans l'Ouest   dans la grande prairie à perte de vue   y'avait ben d'la place assez pour tout l' mond'   pis en fin de compte   y'en pouvait p'us   y'a arrêté sa* job *au* land titles office   his heart gave way   one took the land the other was taken

Mom's *Maman*

eyes bewildered   stroke struck and propped up fatly   she sits on her narrow bed in a narrow room as our sad Mom brushes her long dishevelled hair   we three good little girls in our Sunday best in this stuffy curtains-drawn sick room watch   the only sound a half suppressed sigh   as if Mom had been crying a long time   as she takes that one last look we take leave

disappears

after she dies that *Mémère* is rarely talked about it's as if she just disappeared except for the occasional rushed hushed conversations when *Maman* was mentioned bits of gossip about *Pépère* just putting his wife in a home and leaving her there to die alone because the doctor had said there was nothing more to be done imagine that one daughter-in-law says but he was there for his brother Jess *son bras droit* always consulted him for everything all the wife gave him was fourteen kids and another story had it that as a girl *Mémère* was full of fun and why is it all the good ones die young

la survivante

the prairie
stops her short
freezes
her sea air
island heart
mid beat

and she falls into a deep rut
in the   trundle   trundle
of the pioneer's trajectory

where harsh and stark stay   grey
like dust in white cottons
laundered in hard water

this *Mémère*
never settles in   always
sits on the edge of her chair
scared stiff   as if it were
only yesterday
she stepped off the train
from *Montréal*

saw the big empty

saw that one wet wagon wheel track
in the mud   leading to   nowhere

got swallowed by

all that space   by

a nothing that

wallows in the mouth

balloon

Mémère's face always watchful something could happen a chimney fire a drowning a heart attack a storm a drought the neighbour hanging himself poor man not quite right from fighting at the front and jealous not wanting anybody near his wife and keeping one's mouth proper watching your words *quand on échappe les paroles on n'sait jamais où qu'i' peuvent lander* and eating sparingly you could run out of food have to keep some for *les passants* eat with your mouth closed always taking small bites and small slightly slurpy sips of piping hot tea and keeping your mouth clean wiping it with a homemade Five Roses flour bag serviette many times patting your mouth dry free of crumbs and saliva sometimes i felt a burst of light behind her face that she might cluck or guffaw but she didn't burst spit out didn't drool even a bit this guffaw is a balloon stuck in my chest i want to explode it

violon

the funny thing about my Dad is he has the softest breath and can whistle so sweetly when he isn't mad   like on Christmas Eve when we play carols on the record player that oldest brother and sisters bought for the family   Dad whistles as he sits and reads   Mom likes to tell us he just picks up a tune and when they were still newlyweds   in their unfinished farm house that Dad built   how she'd bought him a violin for his birthday   that March had been so mild   they could even sit outside   Mom said   and later we keep the violin in Mom and Dad's bedroom and sometimes on Sundays when one of the little boys crawls under the bed and fetches it and takes it out of its velvet lined case and hands it to him   and we all coax enough   Dad slowly rubs *arcanson* on his *archet* then glides out the tunes   he knows only two songs completely and just parts of others   how i long   a longing as gold and sharp as the smell of rosin   for him to have continued his violin lessons   even after he got rapped on the knuckles by the nun for being late to his lesson   and that had been it *Mémère* told us   *Pépère* would not tolerate anyone hitting his children   not ever

Mom's rituals

moi, j'ai un régime Mom declares repeats this with her every deft gesture   morning she sponge bathes in a basin of warm soapy water washes her face then scrubs under arm pits with Lifebuoy soap   also washes "down there" with the same vigour   sniffs each armpit again to check for the faintest *trace de sueur*   slides on deodorant   pats talcum powder   girdles and bras herself zippers and buttons up   leaves nothing flopping   places her black hair between wet fingers inserts wave clips   once a week shaves her legs with sure strokes   makes beauty potions shaking glycerine and rosewater in a jar   keeps it on the kitchen counter   tamps it on her face rubs it into her garden worn hands after cleansing them with lemon rind and clipping her nails   keeps those short and filed   polishes them only for weddings   after Dad dies grows her nails as long as talons   and when she's dating again paints them outrageous red   passion purple   pearl pink   lets her hair turn silver softer   every morning after Mom applies her lipstick takes that one last look in the mirror   day begins

mother-in-law

Mom thinks grandmother wears old woman clothes   her and her patched-up big-bosomed grandmother bras   grandmother dresses and grandmother bloomers a grandmother cardigan and a big bib apron   grandmother stockings with crooked seams in the back   bunched up at the ankles above brown lace up shoes   to go get her mail she sports her cream coloured tam   a teal woollen coat   plus she stuffs her purse in a bag   in a bag   in a bag   in three brown paper shopping bags! At home grandmother shuffles in grandma slippers   and in grandma slippers are grandma bunions   at night she dons a large flannelette nightgown then slowly brushes her long silver hair which every morning she knots up in a bun   inserting last her fussy hair net   after the plain brown plastic combs   *la belle-mère's* hair won't obey   won't obey   it always slips out the sides   it won't stay   it won't stay

le déluge

one time the young French teacher with the funny accent who came all the way from *l'Acadie* brought a carload of girls to Winagami Beach after school for a treat   there was a cloudburst and we just made it to the car before it came spilling down like *le déluge*   soon Teacher's green car with-the-windows-all-fogged-up seemed sunk in deepest ocean and i shut my mouth tight   tried not to breathe   but loud sloppy sobs loosed themselves anyway from deep down in my belly   my big sisters and their friends were embarrassed   the girls wanted to show that they trusted Teacher   but i knew Teacher was scared too   she just acted brave   the way adults always try to pretend they aren't worried when they are   that everything is okay when it isn't   i'd heard Teacher crying in the girl's bathroom at school the week before   in the cubicle next to mine   right after morning recess when i'd snuck in to pee when i wasn't supposed to   i never told anyone   there were things about adults that you just didn't bring up especially when you were where you weren't supposed to be in the first place

telling

after singing in *le festival de la chanson française* Mom took the ditch with all the kids in the car   except for the babies who had stayed behind *su' la ferme* with *Mémère*   as we left *le gymnase* the whole prairie sky had filled with huge dark clouds and there had been that strange stillness in the air   so heading the first four miles home after the summer squall hits and the windshield wipers have to work hard Mom bends over the steering wheel as if that will get us there sooner   holds it tightly as the car sheers from side to side and to her dismay Dad's shiny blue Chevy that she had just polished rolls slow motion into the ditch   shaking we huddle under a stand of poplars as the oldest brother walks to the nearest farmer's house to get help   our white shoes full of water   our immaculate socks sopping and grey   and the hem of our Sunday dresses soiled   how on the ride home piled on top of one another in the cab of Monsieur Ouellette's old truck the side of my sister's head is bleeding from a small cut and every time the truck sheers she digs her nails into my other sister's thighs and the driver laughs   thinks it's great fun to scare her   when we make it home we are sent to bed after a sponge bath and a cup of hot cocoa as *Mémère* busies herself with washing the soiled clothes hangs them around the wood stove to dry   Mom rolls Dad a cigarette   is extra careful to make it nice and even   Dad smokes and Mom asks us not to tell   i tell my best friend

Père Noël

in winter the milkman comes dressed as a big brown bear   he doesn't scare my sisters and me   like the fire and brimstone priest who always arrives in a snowstorm waving his black cross or fist about shouting words of doom   of hell   then disappears   or like the handsome uncles with shiny wavy hair who arrive unannounced *comme un cheveu sur la soupe* and twirl mom around and make her skirts flounce and hug her too long and speak too loudly and make her beam   the milkman arrives in a flurry   the fairy tale king of his red jingling sleigh who delivers cream-topped bottles with a bright *Bonjour Madame*   and when we hear the clip clop of hooves turn the corner into our yard we run for our parkas ski pants boots toques scarves mitts   looking surprised to see three girls waiting *Monsieur* smiles bows low then lifts us up onto the sleigh wraps us in woollen blankets   but fur around his beaming daughter   as the cutter sails he sings *des beaux cantiques*   the milkman *est le Père Noël!*

mon beau sapin

The
Christmas tree
we want is like the one
on glittery Christmas cards
properly *pointu égal et
bien branchu.*
Piled up in the old International
we drive up to *une talle d'épinette*
and look and look for this tree.
The oldest brother
gets
to
cut down trees.
The little brothers
walk on crusty snow
sink   to their waists
freeze their feet   cry.
Sometimes the trees are
so sparse we have
to use two to make
one.
That's
when Dad
drills holes in the
trunk, whittles down
bough ends with his *canif,*
re-inserts them so it doesn't
show at all.
One
year Mom
spots the perfect tree.

And she won't let Dad
trim the one uneven branch that juts out like a long arm.

au feu

Sirois's garage
is up in flames and
before we know it
fire gobbles it up
faster than water can
quench. The adults
become small play
figurines with stiff arms
and heads going side to side
repeating, repeating
C'est-tu terrible! Pauvr' lui!
The owner paces and cries.
Can't salvage a thing. Not
a thing! His old mother serves
tea and coffee to those who
have come to help, smiles
through tears, through strained lips.
His father is almost not there
stock still in his rocking chair.
The next day loss hangs around
the village like the smell
of smoke, of soot, like ghosts

patinoire

on a small pond by our house on the other side of the tracks my big brother pulled me   patiently   gently   at the end of his black-taped hockey stick until my wobbly legs held and my small black skates glided jaggedly   later on at the village's open air skating rink i learn to make smoother circles master the art of skating backwards   then when i am old enough to go out alone with two pairs of woollen socks stuffed in my hand-me-down fancy skates draped over my skinny shoulders i walk over to *la patinoire*   after doing the supper dishes   a few steps into the prairie night i can already hear the cold cluck of the puck   the slap shots   the scratch of blades on ice gouging the surface as the guys practise hockey   stop   change directions fast   thud each other's bodies *sur les bandes*   rattle hockey sticks with click-click-clicks   with insistent shouts "Over here! Over here!"   then comes what i like best   free skating   the great arena of the sky over the oval space of the rink and the fresh air and the smell of wood smoke and how on snowy nights as i lie on the ice i get swallowed up by the deep dark blue   as the fluffy falling flakes spin   slow motion   waft me up   up   make me a star

free skating

little kids crisscross
the whole skating rink
helter-skelter
sometimes twist an ankle
in the gouges
on the ice surface   fall
wail out a few measures
for good measure   get up
tears and snot freezing
on their apple-red cheeks
keep on skating
until their feet go numb
pre-teens play crack-the-whip
skate circles around the little ones

la cabane

meanwhile inside
la cabane d'la patinoire
the teens gather
some don't come to skate
but to stoke fires
in the shack sparks fly
and not just in the pot-bellied stove
teens come to smoke
to say and do forbidden things
to sin   out of adult reach
the big guys hold girls' feet
under the guise of helping to lace skates
tickle soft places   mock-twist ankles
big girls squirm   sweaters lift
expose midriffs   parts of lacy underwear
sometimes guys tie skates too tightly
and have to start all over
eyes linger on eyes   on ankles
on crotches   on breasts
some girls luxuriate in the glow
return longer-than-acceptable-
for-good-Catholic-girls smiles
others *les saintes-nitouches*   scandalized
leave in a huff
don't want to hear off-colour jokes

and late at night when
little feet have thawed
tears have soothed
and raging hormones have
played themselves out

inside *la cabane*
inside the cooling stove
sparks transmute into ashes
outside   smoke stops puffing
out of the chimney

hush ya hush ya
all fall down

honey

on a clear day   *nez fin* at the ready for summer scents in the sun-warmed air   Mom whiffs a sharp sweetness   catches a faint buzzing sound   follows its drone into the dankness of the old farm house   a thrum underfoot half startles her and quick with the crowbar she pries out floorboards   discovers a cache of honey   hungry to stake her claim she dons a beekeeper's hood and gloves   fumigates   watches the bees go drowsy   fall   then pillages the whole hive and   victorious   holds the glistering globule high in front of our admiring eyes   extracting her gold in a cast iron pot she skims the cream-like wax   gives us gobs to chew to mould   pleases our eager mouths with slabs of honeycomb   hums as she fills jars storing the sweet opulence of clover for winter   that whole day her smile   her words   her joy   honey

champ de patates

picking

picking potatoes has to be done in one day   long rows of frost-bitten *plants de patates gluants* pulled by hand then dug with hoes   one year the oldest brother digs the rows pulling a borrowed homemade potato digger behind the tractor   we throw a lot of damaged potatoes around that year   as far as we can   aiming at the creek at each other   one lands on *Mémère* on the side of her head   it's the closest we've seen her to getting angry   ever   her eyes go almost black as she mutters picks up her glasses from the dirt inspects them for breakage and places them back   intact   squarely on her nose   nose to the grindstone   even with Mom's insistence she won't leave the field   won't quit   insists on staying pushed by the old fear of starving   our family field day always ends the same way with the drive back to the village twine-tied gunny sacks loaded in the box of the old International followed by the DeSoto full of dirty tired kids with Mom overseeing the dragging of *les poches de patates* into the bin *dans la cave* and scrubbing the dirt-caked kitchen floor on hands and knees as our bathwater steams up the kitchen

help

that last year the parish priest comes to help   instead of his cassock and collar he is dressed in khaki casuals carries a six pack of coca cola   for adults only   which includes the oldest brother and we see Mom tighten around that   but she drinks   receives *le Révérend Père's offrandes* as if it doesn't matter as if he's really helpful   we watch   are allowed to secretly hold contempt

reward

when Dad returns from the Esso café with cartons of pop   bricks of vanilla ice cream   cigarettes   we get to concoct our own floats let orange purple white brown fizz spill over sides of tall glasses   slurp with straws   burp

running water

how when Mom looks out the window   most desirous   and invokes the god of water not just any water *mais l'eau courante*   i conjure it   will a whole field of water   right there in our backyard   just for my Mom   a field like a freshly rinsed ice block just fished from the ice house with steel tongs and rinsed   except that it's liquid and shimmering in the sun   aqua   an abundance of glorious water   just for her   so she can turn on the magical taps and hear the sound of water run and run and run and not be afraid of running out   *mon Dieu   donnez-moi l'eau courante* not be afraid

le bain du samedi soir

Saturday night   early   that's when we take our bath   before *Le Ranch 680* au *Poste CHFA* that makes *les parents* sit and relax   Dad reads through it   he always reads through everything muttering to himself in his deluxe vibrator chair   the tin tub is set on the kitchen floor by the oldest brother   water from the pond or from melted mounds of snow is heated in boilers over two burners on the kitchen stove   steam rises around Mom's face as she tilts the half-full canners   as decanted water sings on the tub's bottom   water which she cools down with a few dippers from the wood-lidded barrel in the porch   two inches   that's as full as our bathtub ever gets to bathe seven kids   the girls get to go first   we wash each other's hair with Lux Soap   rinse with pitchers of water from the tub bottom   then share our damp towels with the boys   it's our job to wash all those little brothers   fish them from the tub legs bent at the knees goose-bumped and trembling soak up the water from their round crew cut heads   rub them down help slip on cotton shorts under flannelette pyjamas   i sometimes clown with them after the bath   become one of *les plus jeunes*   choreograph silly dances *à la musique des rigodons*   we twang elastics   jig to make Mom laugh   Dad doesn't see   he's behind one of the magazines from his pile of Record Gazettes Saturday Evening Posts Popular Mechanics   the older ones if they are still at home waiting for dates or calls act disgusted tell us we we're overdoing it   we don't care   i never see my oldest brother bathe   we call him The King   he has his own room   his very own transistor radio   and before i know it a car too   then he's gone

la fille

my sisters have already started school   are used to other children   are forced to stay inside to watch us through the window   i was sent outside to play with *la fille* because we are the same age   i stand a ways from her   *la fille* is crying   i see her *bottes de rubber* first   black boy's boots!   she's hiding her head in her hands   kicking at a dirty patch of ice underneath the living room window   her *papa* has just left her for the first time   wants her to be with *un autre enfant de son âge* before we go for our first half day of school   soon the girl senses an audience of three   begins to make faces and my sisters laugh as *la fille* lifts her filly head runs in circles her unkempt mane flying   *la fille* doesn't have to wear a jacket   have to wear socks in her boots   i am buttoned up in *mon linge bien propre et repassé*   held   bridled   reined in *moi la fille bien élevée*

school

i sit for the beginning of learning   i am in grade one now going to the new school a new white building that smells of nothing   unlike the musty cluttered *sous-bassement poussiéreux du vieux couvent* or *les odeurs de mon p'tit bois tout à moi*   set above the new green board a white on green alphabet   on top of that hangs a crucifix and beside the classroom door presides a framed black and white photo of young Queen Elizabeth and Prince Philip   and at the back for *la Maîtresse* sits a big round clock   electric   not ticking   not tocking   i learn to sit quietly *en regardant en avant*   i learn not to look around at other children   not out at the waves of ripening grain   not into the wind dancing in the poplar leaves   not up at the puffy shape shifting clouds   i feel the angle of unopened windows the tension of blinds rolled up tightly   on each desk sits a workbook with straight lines to write *la réponse* in between as *Ma Soeur* goes up and down the rows   corrects   corrects   comments on good work   i spot *une faute*   erase it with a bit of *ma salive*   rub rub rub until there is almost a small round hole in the smudged immaculate page   then when *Ma Soeur* who smells of chalk and Lifebuoy soap swoops over my desk in her layered black fabric to check my work asks "Did a little mouse come for a visit?"   her red red X's begin a barbed wire fence in my brain as her chapped holy hand attends to the precision of   check mark   check mark   check mark

common sense

my Dad is the champion of common sense   he knows just the way things are supposed to work   has respect for things   he keeps Mom's good knives sharpened so they slice properly   and they're dangerous so kids are not to touch those   and they are not to be used to cut cardboard   ever or to scrape mud-caked shoes   the old blunt knife will do for that   and we are to ask Mom where she keeps it   kids are part of her domain just like her sewing scissors are which Dad keeps sharpened for her   she sews a lot   and makes her own patterns   and we're not supposed to touch those either   but my sisters and i sneak them to cut out new outfits from the catalogues for our paper dolls and my budding designer brother is always using them for his decorating projects

and tools   Dad respects those too   the most   he buys from the Snap On guy who rolls into our yard in his shiny van and parks in front of the garage doors where he always finds Dad working at something   and that's where Dad always keeps his tools   in order   in the big red shiny tool chest   it's just common sense to put a tool back where you can find it when you need it and we don't touch those either unless you're a boy and think you'll become a mechanic and learn after being shown once how to use a tool properly and can talk about which tool is for what   and we are never to leave a rake out in the rain   things can rust   and it's just foolish   *d'abimer son butin comme ça*   things have to last

les mystères du tiroir à Dad

Dad's drawer is the one above *le* bin *à farine*. Next to where he always hangs the free calendar from the bank. Where he does all his paper work. His drawer is the one closest to the end of the big oak table where his chair is always pulled slightly away, in waiting.

Dad's drawer is sacrosanct, taboo, the line we're just not supposed to cross. He always keeps a receipt book in there. And important papers. And pens, pencils, and a pocket knife to sharpen his pencils. And a roll or two of Scotch Tape.

It is never discovered how the Scotch Tape escapes. And gets used up. But it does. And new rolls have to be purchased. When there's no tape left when he needs it, it makes Dad swear and get red-faced sometimes.

It's the same with the toilet paper. How it disappears! As if it rolls and rolls and rolls away of its own volition. A big case of it never seems to last us. Dad's always having to order more. And when we receive the huge case, he once again gives the instructions how to use it. Properly. And we try. For one sitting or so, then forget.

It's different with Mom's stuff. We all know where the bread and soup go. There's no mystery to that. And the Sunday roast beef and potatoes and gravy, the pies, the chiffon cakes with seven minute icing, the homemade ice cream, and marshmallows, the dozens of doughnuts, the matrimonial cake.

Mom's always there. Even when we've pushed too hard and she raises her arms up in exasperation   says, "That's it! I'm leaving! For good this time!"

infection

a good thing *Mémère* and Mom don't know   they don't want us anywhere near that creek   and Mom has a terrible *peur de l'eau* because two of her brothers drowned in the same lake while working *dans le Grand Nord*   we are creek jumping   *les plus grands* include me show me how to use one of the garden rakes as a pole vault   to launch myself over the creek and to land in the deep parts   we are having so much fun splashing and the creek water is still so cool i don't notice that i'd landed on one of the rake's tines pierced the skin between my little toe and the other toe and twenty-four hours later my foot gets swollen twice the size it usually is   and i'm burning with fever   there's mud packed in there   my god   and that makes Dad really mad and i have to be brought to the hospital and have to stay for a whole week i've never been away from home and the old lady in the bed next to mine tells me to shut up when i cry when no one comes during visiting hours because there's been so much rain that whole week part of the highway got washed out   the funny thing about my Dad is he can't stand people hurting themselves   or much pain at all   and especially accidents   the way that goddamned Pepsi generation drive their cars nowadays burning rubber in the hospital parking lot or speeding along country roads with the headlights turned off playing chicken as if cars are midway rides   or the misuse of implements   like the time my little brother was learning how to walk and picked up a sealer jar that hadn't been put away and it broke because he fell and one of the sharp glass shards sliced off the tip of his nose and Mom glued it right back on and held it tight and steady until she and Dad made it to the hospital for stitches   and that time   after the stitches   how Dad took the axe to the goddamned useless step the baby had tripped over

blue

Dad is mad and slams the truck door   *ma p'tite main fourée partout* is in the way and when he sees that my hand was there he curses and that sure stops my crying   sucking sound back i almost black out   the only thing stopping me a dull tummy ache   i lean against a rigid chest   Mom's   we've been to *Mémère's* after the harvest after closing the farm house for the winter and there's always trouble then arguing and going there makes the adults too mad   a mad that makes you brick up your heart and mortar it the way the throb of your small swollen hand is clutched in by one straight blood-stitched seam   the way he holds hell in his wild eyes   that he can't say i'm sorry   that my mother holds me and.herself in that silence   not to tip the balance   not to explode the goddamned dam

boîte à bois

Dad falls in *la boîte à bois* and can't get out and we are so scared he's had a heart attack   Mom can't pull him out   and has to leave us alone   to get *le voisin*   and the men laugh because Dad is deadweight and it takes a few tries   and Mom doesn't   she gives them a dirty look because drunk again isn't funny to her and she tells Dad to lie on the cot in the living room not in their bed   tells us we aren't to make noise   and after he's slept it off we know they're making up when she gets his tobacco packet with the slice of green apple in it to keep it moist   allows him to hug her and his eyes are sheepish as Mom says *bois pas*   how   not long after that   all hell breaks loose between him and *mon oncle* Paul over things not getting done on the farm   Dad can't get up in the morning because he reads half the damned night and *Mémère* coming into the bedroom to try to get him up   and even if this tussle is the first it's the last Mom says   she's leaving   and to prove it she starts for the road with the baby in her arms and we all hold our breath   after that Dad stops stopping at the bar and we get to move to the village for good   we four oldest are in school already and the yellow bus won't come all the way to our quarter section   and a man tells my Dad he has just the house we need unfinished for only 1300 dollars   it needs work but it's big enough and that price includes two lots

amenities

enfin   Mom *est aux étoiles* as she opens all the windows sweeps the floor and dreams   i can see it in her eyes that she is happy   excited happy   because of the way she sweeps like she means business and dances all at the same time   and she lays the most durable linoleum   and she repaints the kitchen chairs and the bench where the little brothers all sit in a row behind the table and the window frames and the baby's high chair   and she sews curtains   and the best is she got her propane stove   Mom loves her propane stove   the way the heat comes on right away even if the pilot light is hard to relight sometimes   and we have electricity *p'us de vieux fanal ni d'lampes à l'huile à remplir* but no running water it hasn't reached our block yet   but we have the pond and only the oldest brother is allowed there because he's old enough to help Mom haul water and gas for the furnace   and he even gets to empty our chemical toilet   we also get the telephone and our number is nine and my best friend's is six and we have to crank the little black crank twice to go through the operator   but at least we don't have a party line because we live in the village and only people on farms have to have a party line and can listen to other people's conversations   and secrets   my friend and i call each other every day so we can decide on a good place to meet   sometimes we pretend we are teenagers and phone Mme Beauchamp's shy boarder and he plays along with us but because his landlady complained the operator calls our Moms   and we have to stop

operator

i get to go to the telephone operator's house once with my sister and her best friend who lives next door   she's a tiny woman just like her voice and she gets her silver hair permed and always smiles   you can hear it when you phone   the way she asks "*Numéro s'il vous plaît?*"   she always keeps her voice the same for everybody and her tiny lace up brown shoes just reach the top rung of the high stool she sits on   i even see her operating   plugging and unplugging extensions   she's really fast   and after i wonder how does she remember all the numbers and imagine her sitting up there around the clock because i overheard she had to be there at all times   for emergencies

the other side of rain

because   when there's a downpour   Mom remembers how good mud feels between the toes she sends us out to run in the ungravelled lane behind our house so we can revel in the changing sky   run wild   get soaking wet in the occasional warm summer rain and sometimes sight a double rainbow   and after we get to wash our feet in a basin of water from the rain barrel and dry them with old towels that are almost ready for *la boîte à guenilles* in the outside porch where our stray mutt   always called puppy   sleeps except when it's colder than minus thirty   then he's allowed in the inside porch where we keep a big deep freeze that Mom finds so handy because she doesn't have to can anymore   and we end up with stray cats too   they just appear at our door females especially so kittens come quite regularly   sometimes faster than we can give away

customers

afternoons Mom always perks a big pot of coffee and we know when we get to the churchyard if there will be cinnamon buns too   that's the smell of home and after school and the time when my Dad's customers come in to settle their bills and smoke cigarettes   and sometimes their wives come in for perms or hair cuts   Mom doesn't call these customers though she doesn't have her papers   like Dad she just does hair on the side like the farmer's wife who sells Mom eggs to have her own spending money   the village ladies agree *qu'elle a l' tour avec les cheveux ma mère*   the little brothers get crew cuts *c'est plus propre*   and when we're older Mom agrees to let her three girls have long hair   but the oldest brother gets to go to the barber   he has an Elvis cut and buys his own jet boots   if i could have chosen i would have been a hairdresser Mom often says but adds quickly i got a job at the general store to help my family out   we all helped   and that is where i met Ed   he had the nicest car around

beauties

bien une autre! says my French teacher as i walk into second period on Monday morning after my newly bleached blonde sister has just given her a shock   i'm thrilled to see i've just done it again with my crow black hair and i smirk at what she doesn't know   that there's a *tête rouge* back in our village with hair so red it looks as if a light bulb has been lit in her skull and that we all got done last Saturday afternoon by my Mom

exactly right

we get to make fun of Dad   even Mom does   when we're a bit older even though he is a respected member of council and there's even a plaque on the door of *la salle du Conseil du village* with his name on it to prove it   my Dad calls a spade a spade and can cut through bullshit and people listen to him when he does because he doesn't talk a lot   or for nothing   and my Dad never pretends   and he never   never hurries   and that's the biggest joke about my Dad   *qu'i' est donc* slow   how he blows on parts after he grinds   or sands *i souffl' pis i souffl' encore une autr' fois   pis qu'i   frotte longtemps* because every little piece has to fit exactly right   so the machines he repairs run the way they're meant to and the things he constructs last   like the bench he built from scratch when he was only seventeen when people had almost nothing and had to make their own furniture   and *les belles grandes armoires* that he designed just for Mom with a bin *à farine* that could fit her fifty pound bag of Five Roses flour   and drawers that would always open without a hitch   and doors that wouldn't stand askew   the other funny thing about my Dad is he can spend hours repairing the oldest lawn mower in the world even if it means building a part for it himself   even if it takes two days   it's worth it he tells Mom who gets quite exasperated at times   but in the end agrees it is worth it when that motor starts running   just to see old Zoël's face light up

le rigodon du pain béni

>Back of the bread is the flour
>And back of the flour is the mill
>And back of the mill
>is the wind and the rain
>And the Mother's will

Lundi matin
Ouvr' le bin à farine
Met d' l'eau dans le bol
À faire du pain
Ajoute un peu d' sucre
Saupoudre d' la levure
Mélange le tout avec ta main
Prie la Sainte Vierge
Pour tout ce qu'i' a d'bien
Attends
Ajoute du lard
À c' bon mélange
D'autre liquide
et d' la farine
Brasse le tout vigoureusement
D'autre farine du bin à farine
Vas-y
Creuse tes mains
Dans cette belle pâte
D'autre farine du bin à farine
Fais une boule
Sur le comptoir
Pétris le pain
Le pain maison
D'autre farine du bin à farine
Prie la Sainte Vierge
Pour tout ce qu'i' a d'bon
Attends
Coupe la pâte
Et forme tes pains

*Laisse-les lever
Une deuxième fois
Mets-les au four
Pour la cuisson
Maintenant ça n'sera
Pas long
Mon Dieu que ça sent bon
La communion
N'est bas ben loin   Attends
(Vendredi matin, on recommence tout)*

four squares and "Hey, you!"

he holds the paper
in his left hand and
folds with the right
nice neat Dad folds
folds the end paper
over the second square
the third square
over the second square
and flips the fourth
over the third
all corners aligned
perfectly in pure Dad logic
to make the wad more absorbent
to prevent getting
your hands in "it"
water is scarce
and if you can master
this skill you won't have
to wash your hands after
and the great crates of
toilet paper Dad shops for
won't disappear so soon
how we go through it
how it almost gives him
a nervous breakdown
to hear the roll whiz
out of control on his
homemade wire holder
fastened to the wall
with a spike
little assholes
is all we have
he emphasizes
as he instructs
all his kids named "Hey, you!"
instructs us how to wipe

our asses more efficiently
with no more than
four skimpy squares
of toilet paper
that is all we
little assholes need
claims the Father
heavy with duty

Nom de Dieu!

Dad doesn't use the F-word.
He makes his own swears
like roll-your-own cigarettes.
There is a kind of economy
to that and every blaspheme
comes out differently. In
this one   his favourite   he
inserts Christ right smack
in the middle of the Tabernacle
"*Tabar Chriss de Nac.*" He
says equal emphasis on *ab iss ak*.
In his next favourite he throws
a chalice   in there   creating
his very own Trinity of swears.
"*Calice de Chriss de Tabarnac.*"
And for extreme causes   after
a pause   raises   teeth clenched
a Holy Host   atop these three,
"*Hostie!*" trying to put a full
stop to his fuming.
The holy ghost   a hammer on
a thumb   black blood   trapped
between nail and skin   the
holy ghost   a drill bit twined
in blue black jack shirt aiming
straight for his heart   eyes too
caught up in fear   to find the
God damned switch. Yes in
a pinch English swears will do.
My Dad doesn't discriminate
when calling upon the name
of God in vain.

portrait de noces

aunt Eveline lives in Kelowna   just in the next province *Mémère* insists and where she lives it is close to the land of milk and honey   there are orchards there rows of trees *chargés de fruits* fruit that doesn't grow here in this province of biting cold and *Mémère* wishes and prays and begs for Dad to move the whole family to B.C. because she could grow flowers there and we all know by now that she will never return to Jersey   her friend Blanche who still writes tells her how things have changed   auntie sends things our way on the Greyhound Bus glorious fruit set in purple packaging in wooden crates golden pears and soft rosy skinned peaches   *Mémère* brings back pictures of their outings at a park with a large lake one of her and auntie dressed up sitting under a tree so big they can both lean on it   auntie writes letters and her penmanship is so fine and formal like Dad's like letters from the old country   she sends postcards sometimes   and for the birth of my littlest sister a real fancy card with a cradle that rocks when you open it   auntie makes Mom sour   i don't know why Mom holds her every gift in the cold in the place where nothing grows canning the ripe pears and peaches as if they didn't really come from her   as if they were Mom's idea in the first place   her jars of sweet fruit her crown jewels   Mom takes all the credit and acts as if she wants us to forget auntie's fancy life   the way the tilt of auntie's bridesmaid hat casts a shadow straight across her pretty face on Mom and Dad's wedding picture

toots

mon oncle Paul is *Mémère's* youngest   he has never left home   "he's shy my Paul he's shy" she always says "he has eczema bad"   he can only do odd jobs between seeding and harvesting and grandma is always concocting infusions for him which he mostly drinks when he has scratched enough and his skin's raw   once in a while though he really drinks goes on a toot with bad guys *des voyou*s   men who satisfy each other in the woods behind the bar!   *Mémère* doesn't know that though   my best friend told me   and her brother who is much older and of drinking age told her   *mon oncle* Paul loosens up when he drinks   oh his eyes shine   and his body gives   he does little *gigues pis il turlutte* and weaves and talks to everybody but sometimes his legs can't hold him up real well and he trips all over other Saturday night patrons   so often the bouncer has no choice but to throw him out by the scruff of the neck and *mon oncle* lands rumbling down the steps like a gunny sack full of rocks   afterwards he slinks back to the tiny house he shares with *Mémère* and sleeps it off then rolls cigarettes   fine and slim   and though grandma is relieved to have him back she scolds anyway about smoking   look at those nicotine-stained fingers!   but still she offers him tea with lots of carnation milk in it or instant coffee   whatever he wishes and soup

falling from grace

how i itch for freedom from *mes* pilled *bas bruns raccommodés* held up with knobby *jarretières* it's early spring and the weather is swinging between bitter cold and thawing warm and some ground is showing through it's Friday lean Friday and Lent this means definitely no meat *on doit jeûner* Mom likes it because she gets to prepare easy meals from her repertoire of simple dishes fish croquettes pancakes fried potatoes and eggs with bright yellow yolks she's surprised she's never lost her taste for them she always tells us we ate so many on the homestead Mom sends me to *le magasin général* to buy a dozen eggs before closing time and i sneak my brand new puddlers out from under her bed from the box with beige tissue wrap and slip my feet into the new white bobby socks that she's saving for Easter Sunday fastening the sassy little elastic over the button on the side i am shocked by their redness delighted anew by the light feel of rain boots and i begin to conjure up green grass and warm summer wind but once outside my plastic boots stiffen so fast i'm afraid they'll crack and what then? i fret as i feel each nub of rut each sleek ice patch through the thin soles and my bare knees shake these boots have no grip i buy the dozen eggs use the change for gum what was i thinking anyway it's still too cold for those flimsy boots everybody in the village knows that and i try to hurry it up a bit because Mom is waiting and halfway home i sprawl and skin my knee and half the eggs splatter and Mom instantly sees the damage gives me the sad look says "*Tu me désappointes*" and "we'll have tough pancakes for supper" and "where's the change gone?" with the eggs she supposes

stopped short

with the new baby boy that makes eight   and we think he's the last   he's so pudgy and cute the three girls fight over who will stroll him around the block in his carriage to show him off   Mom is almost always in the kitchen now   cooking feeding the soup pot with a handful of rice with chopped green onions that feel slimy on the tongue with shredded carrots and cabbage   sometimes she adds canned tomatoes   *la grosse chatte* spread eagles on the polished linoleum and out of her backside the beginning of a black bud   Mom quickly retrieves a cardboard box from *la cave* and lines it with *flanelette* rags from *la boîte à guenilles*   gently soothing she *s*coops *la minoune* into the birthing box as we stoop form a ring of heads and   mesmerized   watch her lick each kitten clean and slick   eat the cellophane-like sacs   how the blind newborns mewl crawl find her swollen tits suck   and another day as i am helping Mom make cabbage rolls the ribbed feel of the leaves remind me of my secret   it began with the tone of their laughter which hurt like a rusty ice pick through the guts   a boy and a girl are playing catch with one of the kittens then swinging it and jiggling the swing's ropes   how the skinny thing clings on   it has desperate eyes like *Mémère*'s when Dad swears at her   eyes like Mom's when airplanes fly low overhead trembling the roof and she thinks World War Three is being declared and we don't have a shelter and where will we hide from the bomb   and will my oldest be enlisted

cavities

all this time my mouth is open wide and frozen   cold and dead is what i feel   they are talking over me as if i'm not there   the travelling dentist talks cavities as he expertly assesses the damage "You people, in this neck of the woods,"   backwoods, he means, and he also means *Canadiens français* – frogs   "have too many damned children," and he presses, "You probably feed them rotten meat."   Mom sucks in her breath as if she's been punched hard in the solar plexus squares her shoulders angles her head defiantly.   SHE'S MAD!   "Which one is too much?" Mom wonders out loud. "Which one would you send back?" she retorts   stunned by her own freshness by having talked back to authority   twice   she backs off as the dentist drills and fills   discards the part about the rotten meat

baby sitting

in the neighbour's house where i often babysit stands *un beau meuble* with bevelled mirror doors and a drawer full of shoes   full of fancy going out shoes that are like rare fish in a pool   the sleek-heeled salmon-coloured ones leap out pull me deep into slippery desire i dare not walk in   i slip my feet in anyway teeter a few steps   stop   feel drunk with wish with want with the ache of being in between   in the middle   too old to play with dolls too young to go out with boys not old enough for a real job like the three oldest have   and i'm not allowed to go to hall dances yet either even though a boy cousin my age plays in the Nighthawks Band and his Mom and Dad *mon parrain et ma marraine* always go and watch   how i detest babysitting the blandness of afternoons that stretch out into evenings that feel as long as *le carême*   as slow as March

ma marraine

ma marraine always has a small dog named tiny and she refers to it as *ma p'tite tiny* which we think is funny because it means tiny-tiny   and she kisses her dogs on the mouth   Mom thinks it a bit strange that she likes her dogs so much because Auntie Em likes a clean house and one that stays that way too and according to Mom dogs are dogs and belong outside   *et pis j'endurerais jamais un chien dans ma maison* Mom declares *y'a ben assez des chats qui font du poil partout*   so when *Pépère*'s *deuxième femme* Madame Caron invites *les trois jeunes filles* on a trip to to visit Auntie Em in Dawson Creek Mom instructs us to be polite   because Madame has never had children   and it will take a long time because *Pépère* doesn't drive any faster than thirty miles an hour and to take our shoes off at the door as soon as we get to auntie's house   she keeps it so spotless you could eat off her floor   and when we finally arrive i notice that auntie likes a lot of matching stuff   like toothbrush and tissue holders   *serviettes de bains et débarbouilletes*   and she has a lot of *bibelots* and it is whispered *qu'elle est pas mal dépenseuse   même extravagante   a' veut toujours du nouveau*   the latest   *pis a pouva' êtr' dur su'son pauvre' Jean   mais a' l'aima don'*   but *tout ça c'ta peut-êtr' juste des entendus dire   parce que ma marraine* she liked fun   how she laughs as she reminisces about how she and my Mom would giggle during prayer services at *le pèlerinage de Girouxville*   and how they would take long walks   *sur les* tracks   two newly-weds with their arms around each other's waist *des belles-soeurs*   with the rest of their lives in front of them

des belles noces

la mariée wears a cream-coloured bridal gown and fairy tale shoes *imagine toé q'elle a même r'couvert ses souliers elle-même pour matcher sa robe* she appliquéd flowers from leftover wedding gown fabric even sheathed the heels with pieces of satin cut from in between the flowers   Oh! thank God it wasn't raining that day!   *pis qui qu'y aurait cru qu'une vieille fille pis un vieux garçon auraient pu trouver leur* match   just like that *tout d'un coup* they found each other   it happened so fast *et pis qui qu'y aurait cru qu'elle aurait fait une si belle mariée une mariée si éblouissante*   elle qui éta' toujours pas mal échevelée   who would a' thought   *qu'y'avaient donc l'air heureux pis que c'était beau à voir   et pis que ça tu fait des beaux portraits de noces sur les marches*   coming out of *l'Eglise du Sacré Coeur* at mid-day there they were *le couple parfait* two tiny figurines on top of a three-tiered wedding cake   the Prince and the Princess and *à l'occasion de leur mariage* the whole village was there watching   in awe

ordination

so much black-robed and surpliced pomp and a professionally baked cake was special ordered from the city   an open book *la Sainte Bible*   iced in an antique green sheen and trimmed in gold with a cluster of fake purple grapes on it   so life-like and plump   one of the big girls helping out can't resist pinches one off plops it into her mouth and slowly licking her lips savours the sweetness then with her saliva-wet finger re-smoothes out the surface to restore the effect of perfect   and the eyes of the village women and girls   wide   in this same church basement starved for *des occasions spéciales* to move out of hum drum to flutter fawn over flush with excitement   every woman there has secretly hoped and prayed *pour une vocation dans la famille afin d'êtr' sauvé*   oh for her own son priest   but to touch the hem of his robe   *imagine toé* says one to the other *ça y'a pris sept ans d'études au séminaire* he must be very smart   nothing like the life of married woman   how she swells   births   bleeds   lactates   drips   prepares formula   spoons mushed up food in small spitty mouths   rinses diapers   soaks them in pails till laundry day   strips bed of pee-soaked sheets   launders   makes steaming pots of soup   washes floors   blows noses   wipes tears   empties slop pails   and at the high point of the ritual flanked by bishop archbishop and prominent priests the ordained one lowers himself into a full body prostration kisses the ground and then a banquet is held in his honour served by the village women and girls   for Him the accomplished beloved good son we get to sneak sips of the leftover wine

small white coffins

a church full of *paroissiens* in their winter coats   the smell of wool and bleached handkerchiefs   the sound of muffled sobs   the mother's grief a grief with no relief frozen in her face as she bends over her baby's small white coffin at the front of the church   how he had gotten hold of the wintergreen bottle that she had used to make a batch of Christmas candy that she had forgotten to put away   and the gossip only dug deeper about how her little ones were left *tout seuls* too often every morning *pendant qu'elle allait aider aux hommes à faire le train   y'a des femmes qui aiment mieux travailler dehors qu' être dans 'a maison   avec leurs p'tits tu sais*   and so recently too another mother torn by this same sorrow   *elle l'a perdu de vue juste pour deux minutes   son p'tit*   and as she ran outside ran for the tracks she knew   she already knew   and screamed and gestured to flag down the conductor to stop the train *tout c' temps-là* seeing her youngest being bumped and thumped under a rolling train   and the conductor just waved back

marionnettiste

on the kitchen counter sits our cardboard box full of picnic food: potato salad mayonnaise washed leaf lettuce vinaigrette homemade hot dog buns bulk wieners   sandwiches made from leftover roast beef French's mustard relish homemade pickles matrimonial cake last autumn's canned fruit from the Okanagan Kool-Aid packets lidded pitchers Melmac dishes cutlery tea towels dish soap and a basin for the washing up   the diaper bag bursting with baby clothes and formula slumps by the porch door each child is ready   and waiting   bathing suit under summer holiday clothes towel wrapped around small neck   baby has been fed naps in Mom's arms   it is a sunny going-to-the-beach Sunday   on such days after High Mass there is a veritable exodus which we sometimes join but mostly not   the smell of dust in the air from this sudden burst of traffic fills the kitchen as we wait the eight of us   nine with mom   to load up the car   Dad is deep in reading again   bent over his end of the big table   mumbling   two of the little brothers get restless   on the verge of whiny   and Mom the expert *marionnettiste* sends the first signal to Dad who grunts looks up dazed returns to his text   a few more tugs "Ed? Ed?" unglues him from the table's edge and   still blank-eyed   Dad makes his exit to check the car   we keep our ears peeled for the sound of the DeSoto motor   pray he doesn't find something major   we do all but applaud when peering through the window we see the oil can in his hands   know by now that this   though a slow enough process for our Dad   does not entail major repair   we should make it to the beach only two hours later than everybody else this time   rather than not at all other times   Dad's face contorts as he repairs   repairs on Sunday   *la journée du Sabbat*   his only day off   and he has to be bringing kids to the beach   when we get to go we know to sit quietly like angels   like saints   and there will be no kid's head or arm or hand waggling out of car windows   remnants of despair float among us like the smell of dust settling over the village after all the other families have left   for a whole day at the beach

accordéon

my sister's sometimes friend one of the wild ones   one of those the adults call *une p'tite gouine*   comes over brings her accordion takes it out of the case and right away right away i know down there   deep down   that we're on the brink   on the brink of something new   of audacity   like a mouth full of white actress teeth coming out of a big-glossy-red-lips smile   like a too-low *décolleté*   like teetering on high high sling backs   the ivory keys   smooth slick   the black buttons the folds   how they breathe as she slips her hands through the straps adjusts herself and the accordion   then she starts to play   i start   am baffled   this music blooms   "blooms" down there   full like peonies in June   fills my belly the way the smell of roses or hyacinths can fill a room with too much perfume   makes me stifle a laugh so powerful   dangerous   seems like a dam will burst like a tire with too much air in it   i want something sharp to release the pressure   and she sings too!   that's when i run upstairs because her face is like the face on the calendar girl uncle Paul has on the wall beside his single bed a lady wearing a red off-the-shoulders chiffon dress that looks as if it will disintegrate like a mantle on a lantern if you touch it   like a moth too close to the flame   you don't touch it   you feel awkward   want something   have a feeling you shouldn't be having

grand raconteur

my best friend's father *est un raconteur et pis quand i' raconte* he insists on displaying all the contents of his cartful of odds and ends every time *"Hey, j'en connais une bonne!"* he begins raucous-voiced like *le corbeau* in *Les fables de La Fontaine*   and we know he's off   that he will pull up joke after joke   some with the punch line still on some not   as he picks   pell-mell through the same old bits and pieces of *ses histoires*   in between cups of Maxwell House Instant Coffee and Macdonald's Menthol Cigarettes   through thick smoke he conjures up a jumble of tall tales from *la Belle Province* mixed up with *contes et légendes* and local lore   displays *avec de grands gestes les dictons* of *Monsieur Un Tel et Madame Une Telle which makes* him sentimental and solemn-voiced as he intones true stories of his glory days singing solos in the church choir for *la messe de minuit*   calls to mind the departed he has known in his glorious past with his long dead first wife   from a very good family   these become *les caractères dans ses histoires*   his second wife some say doesn't count quite as much *i para' qu' est pas toute là   c'est vrai qu' est pas souvent là* she works away as a cook *dans les chantiers*   always he ends with his favourite   the trickster story which makes him chortle then cough   the one about moving *les bécosses la nuit d'* Halloween   how he and *les gars* get to laugh their heads off as some half asleep sucker falls in the shit hole reaching for the door handle in the dark   and dizzy from too much smoking i reach for the tap   fill my glass   and as i'm gulping a nicotine stained paw cups my breast from behind   his daughter's eyes go blank   as if a light switch has been turned off

first kiss

i was asked along   to make it easier for my sister to get permission to go out on a week night   and when the feeling comes back   standing at the kitchen counter doing the supper dishes   she's giving me the talk   something about "the other night" and not getting my hopes up and being still too young   and grief hits me like a brick   i'd tried to put it out of my mind   i'd been walking in a fog that felt more like a slough and as i fought the nausea of a bout of parking   of necking   in a backseat with my sister's boyfriend's friend   and how   suddenly enfolded in gangly arms   i'd gotten suctioned onto lips   my head craned at a neck breaking angle   and it wasn't at all like in the movies all sweet with romantic music in the background   my first kiss had got ruined and it reminded me of the only time i was forced to finish a bowl of lukewarm porridge

swimming lessons

waking in the woods to mottled light in early morning's brief sumptuous quiet i remember that i am at the lake and here i don't have to be tending to siblings or helping with household chores   this is the last summer before i have a real job the last summer i take swimming lessons   i am in a big converted bus with my best friend who is real grown up and who doesn't like to rough it   she dislikes the lake water and the sun one is too cold the other too hot   i both envy and hate her "maturity" *ses cheveux bien placés son déodorant* her prim and proper pressed clothing and that she has had her periods for a number of years already   mine have just come but nobody knows that   and she gets to drive but i don't Dad doesn't lend his car doesn't want to start that   my best friend keeps the bus spanking clean runs it like a household gets to make all the rules because the bus belongs to her father so we know to toe the line most of the time except when the water fights break out   then sand gets trailed in which gives her the perfect excuse to be oh so efficient do the wiping up with *les guenilles* she had packed in case and handing out extra towels she also thought to pack for emergencies and to look down at us like an exasperated mother ever so fond of her hard-to-manage-brood   come dusk beach friends congregate in the bus   no one uses sun block so some are more red than others   the slow oncoming darkness makes us all equal smoothes down the day's differences as we slip into pyjamas behind makeshift change rooms of held up beach towels move into appointed sleeping slots unroll sleeping bags adjust pillows bed down   a new feeling floats up like a bubble from the slough bottom like a lily pad blossom rooted somewhere deep and mud sucky that makes the body come alive   hands slip out of sleeping bags   nudge shoulders   edge close to breasts   grope and hold back all at once like that first-of-the-season walk in the lake when the water level gets higher than your bathing suit line   cold hits your back   you walk on tiptoes   hold your breath

relax

the funny thing about my Mom is when she started smoking menthols and it was a doctor who told her to he was even a specialist it was after the last three surprises were born which now made eleven of us the three oldest had jobs already and were leaving home and now i got to be the oldest and to take care of the kids and the house Mom went to the city for this appointment to a throat doctor who couldn't find a thing wrong with her said everything looked pretty good down there so he asked her some more questions like how many kids do you have? eleven seven boys four girls she said and he said no wonder your throat is always sore you must scream a lot which made Mom start a bit do you smoke? he inquired oh no she said well lady i think you need to relax so just sit down after every meal and have a cigarette so that's what she did that's when i tried my first cigarette at home that is i wanted to show off for my oldest brother and made a perfect smoke ring and he said that girl's been smoking for some time my oldest brother was like that he could tell those things

truck stop

loaded down with an order i accidentally spill milk on a snobby lady's fur coat   a woman from the rival village   tight-lipped   the woman just looks at me scornfully   utters *pauv' p'tite niaiseuse*, sniffs indignant   wipes the milk off her fur with a hanky from her gold-clasped city-bought black purse *et Merci Dieu* that the damage isn't worse   she waves me away like she would a pesky fly   i pick up a lot of Saturday night shifts because my sister who has all the curves is popular and is going steady and i'm not i get stuck with the bar rush and all these orders slurred at me and the drunken jokes fired every which way   and i paralyze sometimes   like the time this really popular guy blasphemes *ma Chriss!* trying to chase away a fat fly burbling over his sugar bowl and i think he's swearing at me and just stand there order pad poised not letting on   and the first thing i know his gaze moves to my chest   probes through my polyester uniform as he exclaims *tabarnac t'as pas de jos toé* and orders a hot beef sandwich all in one breath   and when the cook finds me crying in the walk in freezer   asks *quossé qui t'as dit c'grand frais chié là*   how she howls with laughter when i tell her   says *t'inquiète pas ma fille si y'en aurait un dans la gueule i pourra' pas chanter O Canada!*

clean up duties

after the bar rush we get to clean the Esso café   make it spic and span for the after-church Sunday crowd   we all pitch in end with sweeping then mopping up the muddied floor   and sometimes after we're all done we make ice cream sandwiches and down one more free pop real fast before locking up   there's clean up duty by day too   eight deep-fryer-greasy-floor-to-ceiling windows to wash balanced on top of a pop crate on top of a wobbly café table and we have to do them the proper way which means   *un bon savonnage   un rinçage à l'eau chaude   un rinçage au vinaigre*   and we get to dry them with good cotton rags until our arms feel as if they'll fall off   all this under the surveillance of Monsieur Édouard who has been a military man   who thinks it's still his job to oversee that everything is well organized and neat and tidy   to pride himself on finding something not done and turning abruptly in a huff and doing it himself   then delivering yet more precise doses of scorn commands the chip stand the candy stand the pop cooler the cigarette slots are to be kept full   full at all times   the cream pots washed and replenished before the milk goes sour   necks of ketchup bottles un-gummed   sugar bowls refilled   counters and tables wiped clean and gleaming

summer of '66

come summer there are milkshakes to shake   thick and lumpy   vanilla strawberry chocolate banana   and on real hot Sundays floats to concoct   and for hours i dig out scoop after scoop after scoop of ice cream for single and double and triple-decker cones   get the front of my blue polyester uniform all gummy with wax from inside the five gallon containers confettied with multicoloured drips from all the flavours from dipping and dipping the stainless steel scoop in hot water i am a rock i am an i-i-island

Ca-na-da! and burn your bra!

in his homily weasel-voiced little Father Spinach   as my brothers called him in secret   had delivered the Church's latest decree on birth control   *c'est*, he'd pontificated *le devoir de toutes les femmes de renouveler le berceau à toutes les années.*   and my sisters and i think doesn't he know women are burning their bras?   and this is 1967?   but we don't say a thing   thank God   because Mom is so mad   when she comes home from church she's swearing a blue streak and the roast is burning and we are all hungry and she doesn't care   *parce que là 'est ben décidée* there'll be no more rocking the cradle   no more buns in the oven   no more rhythm method   i'm done! she shouts   as if she needs the whole neighbourhood the whole world   to know   still in her newest home-tailored going-to-mass suit she'd bypassed the kitchen thrown her purse on Dad's chair and had started pounding the coffee table   hard   as she spat out what does he know about *être en famille lui*? and of having that baby?   and she even calls him *p'tit trou de cul*   he has *de l'audace* to preach to me about filling the cradle   and   no i won't complete the dozen for *le centenaire du Ca-na-da! non merci!* she'd blurted out when a friend jokingly suggested this on the church steps after mass   that is not funny   Mom scowled   a twelfth child was not a project centennial year or not   on Monday   *c'était "la pilule"*

spark plugs for God's sake

Sundays the aunts arrive.
Corsetées.   *Toutes bien habillées!*
After lunch.   Always after mass.
In uncle driven cars, maroon or navy blue.
Accost us with shining eyes,
with red, red lipstick kisses,
their too-big smiles showing gums and bridges.

Spread *eau de toilette* scents as they speak.
Laugh. Slap their thighs.
"You don't say!"
"Oh, for God's sake!"
Clip on earrings pinch small stretched lobes.
Well-placed, wave-clipped hair
matches the properness of their posture.

The women in that family do not slump.
Ever.   Sit on straight-backed chairs.
Crossed arms uphold their breasts.
Pointed straight ahead like headlights.

"Spark plugs, spark plugs"
my little brothers call "them".
Run up the stairs,
throw their convulsed boy bodies
onto their beds.
Say it over and over again,
"Spark plugs.   Spark plugs.   Spark plugs."
And laugh, faces sunk in their pillows.

élévateurs

elevators make me think of auntie p
p is for *particulière* and peeved a lot
she was the youngest of fourteen
the one appointed to take care
of her stroke struck mother
but escaped   *a' tombé en famille*
got small wedding   shot gun
wore a navy blue suit   white gloves
white pumps   a small neat hat with a net
a few quick photos taken at the front of the church
click   click   click   the couple looks straight
into the camera as they walk down the aisle   click
toward the back   one on their way out   click
film all done   that's it   wedding's over
no honeymoon   and hush hush of
maybe baby   bun in the oven
mon oncle pis ma tante start a life
une vie de couple une vie dure
the wife of the grain elevator man
the uncle who always jangles a
lot of loose change in his pockets
the tall taut quiet one who drives a
Volkswagen Beetle
never could figure out how
his long long legs would fit
loved his rye   brayed like an ass
when he would finally laugh
let us ride on his feet if we bugged
enough   climb on his head too
steal the loose change that spilled from his pockets
behind the couch cushions as we play wrestle
his slick pitch black hair always stayed put
his blue eyes   waters that run deep   but
so far away   nobody can really   see
him   nobody ever   allowed there

two uncle Als

the tall tall one is *un agent d'élévateur* this makes him so important have status be at the hub Mom says it's too bad he has good employment but but he often argues with customers and even his supervisors that's why they have to move around so much get "transferred" a lot and every time *qu'i' déménagent* auntie has to start all over the short one likes to play the part of a joker he's a roly poly of a man never figured out what he did for a living but he sure could cough when he laughed never got transferred that one stayed put put-put-puttered around his property rented rooms i think maintained his place as head of the household quite a squat home his domain if i remember well married quite a young thing *vingt ans plus jeune que lui* and made it abundantly clear that *le boudage* would be inadmissible a wife of his would never do that pouting is the one thing he would not tolerate had seen enough of it *dans d'autres mauvais ménages* and you know who we mean not that he was one to talk about others but still we have to keep things straight and at the end of the month all the columns have to balance down to the last penny we have to keep accountable and never serve more than one kind of vegetable and just a small bowl of peas at that

ma tante Eva's ways

the way you told jokes   always the same jokes   and we'd never miss Carol Burnett   the stopped-breath way you laughed   covered your loud puffy Ah! Ah! Ah's   the way you managed boarders in your small row house after *mon oncle's* series of heart attacks   the way you two took the bus to W.W. Arcade   walked arm in arm to get groceries uncle trailing the little cart behind him   the way you went to *la coiffeuse* once a week coiled toilet paper around your do every night   the way you maintained a routine   laundered on Monday   shopped on Tuesday   baked bread rich deserts giant cookies and tried out new casseroles on Wednesday   did your *grand ménage* on Thursday   saved Friday and Saturday for out of town guests who always arrived unannounced   mostly *de la parenté*   the way you walked to *la Basilique Saint-Joseph pour la messe du dimanche*   the way every afternoon no matter what you closed your lined front room curtains   watched your soaps *As the World Turned*   how you fretted over the characters' lives as if   they were your own children   *Mon Dieu* the acting is so lifelike!   the way you worried about *mon oncle's* heart when he watched wrestling on TV how he got in that ring with the wrestlers   the way your bread didn't rise like Mom's and made your house smell slightly yeasty   the way hearing your back-and-forth steps on the cracked linoleum of your small north-facing kitchen with the spindly spider plant sheltered me like a heart beat

the ascension of *ma tante Bartine*

my aunt has died   the one who got   king size headaches   the one who saw red   the thin slender-legged one   the blue-eyed one with an actress face   she was never happy that one nothing could satisfy her they all said   she smoked started young they said   drank too   wore big bejewelled clip-on earrings   left uncle   i wonder who left who   she'd been dying for twenty years had no stomach left   or was it liver   to speak of   we don't know how she survived that long   it's a miracle they all said even her children   when she never died when she was supposed to   she hung on till the end   six weeks of hanging on as if to a thin filament   the way you used to drag on those cigarettes auntie as if they were your very breath your lifeline   what a rebel you were from the very beginning they all said yeah   isn't it too bad   and of course you had to work where they served liquor   where there would be men   you with that fancy purse   with your bangs all in kiss curls   not too many people could get away with that but you could   that's how pretty and daring you were   your hair a rich brown and your eyes sapphires made of dawn and dusk   no hospital kitchen work for you   you with your straight cuts and matching sweater sets   you always looked ready to go out   and sometimes as if you'd been out too late   and you were angry quite a lot of the time as if you didn't understand this thing of having kid after kid   and raising the eight of them   gorgeous you were   and they never said that gorgeous was too dangerous   not the way life is supposed to be lived   lived   all the way

impact

when they arrived *au petit matin* to tell Mom she said "It's Mich isn't it? I knew it   I always knew something would happen to that one!" that was the last time Dad stood up dressed   and walked   to see you in your coffin   you who feared his death the most went and died first   some said you prepared the way for Dad   some whispered that liquor was probably involved   i told myself at least you died doing something you liked – driving around all night in the red Dart Swinger – with someone special   even though she was your best friend's girlfriend   died after building me a fire in your green velour bathrobe   long light hair backlit like an angel's   which you weren't   you died on impact the report said   not so for the girlfriend

Mom's funny ideas

Mom always says when i get old put me in an old folks' home because that's where the old belong   your room is cleaned for you there and your meals are served and the people working there are trained to care for you   and we say Mom why do you say that? we would never do that   i don't want to be a burden on anyone she insists doesn't want to be trouble   and she knows what she's talking about she says because when she'd taken a second job cooking in the nursing home where her *papa* lived his last days   because she needed extra money to buy all the things she wanted for her dream home   she saw how her *papa* was *si net et confortable*   and she even got to serve him *des p'tits spéciales* sometimes like canned tomatoes and toast for supper   and management would let her because he was never any trouble at all and she was such a good worker and never complained about having to wash a pail full of leaf lettuce and agreed to take extra shifts   and she didn't even mind when *Pépère* started to forget even forgot her and spent a lot of time talking to Jess   as if he was there with him and they were back homesteading

found poem 1

what a grand surprise to get your letter! Mom is here for lunch   I want her to mail this   I'm always the same   only weaker   indeed i pray for you dear   do so for me   not much news here   but I expect to move to another home soon   there are nurses there   not here well we have snow today   say hello to your boy pray our Good Lord for my recuperation and all your needs too love in our Savior Jesus Christ
                                  gramma

found poem 2   God is my helmet

I am so thankful to you for getting my letter to Mr. Propp he visited Dad in the hospital and now concerning the favour you desire for praying in thankfulness I am sending you the whole sheet of graces can you type them anew as these words were so touching to you so is my heart filled with gratitude to hear you say you believe them now I know that one of my grandchildren is seeking our solid rock when we are at peace with Him He sees for all our needs the graces are as old as my Bible all this is my strength and my stay without God at the helmet I couldn't advance could be the day is approaching when I will see him face to face today Dad came home for a few hours I gave him my old Bible I pray that he will be in the will of God before the end comes it's a nice warm day we had lots of rain lately I'm so happy over your good letter it brightens my days maybe we'll see you soon every good wishes to you please write again excuse all the mistakes and words left out   my mind wanders   also my hand   Love from Mom and us all   grandma

Notre Père

> *L'âge d'or c'est la mort...*
> *On redevient petit enfant*
> *dans le ventre de la mort.*

Notre père pendant que
sur ton corps s'insinue
le cancer   tes yeux creux
essayent de capter
les images floues
qui grouillent
comme mille petits lézards
sur les murs verts, ternes
de ta chambre d'hôpital;
tes mains effleurent,
tu marmonnes,
et au dernier moment
c'est la maladie qui
te chuchote à l'oreille
"Viens. Ne respire
plus.
Ne respire plus
lâche
lâche
le fil
de ton
souffle"
Et tu nous quittes
docile et petit
dans
ton lit.
Comme
dans
les bras
de ta
Mère.

Our Father

Our father
who art with cancer
hallowed be thy bare bones
thy time has come
your will on this earth
no more will be done
blessed are you and
your last mouth-mutterings
your hollow eyes staring beyond
your soft dying hands sifting through
thousands of details, frayed
end-of-life threads
skittering up and down
dull green hospital walls
like tiny lizards
you are being delivered
into her arms
and what a wondrous
crossing.
Amen.

buns

after Dad died and the last two had gone Mom takes to baking buns   when her two younger sisters visit they bake buns for all occasions   cinnamon buns hot cross buns whole wheat buns oatmeal molasses buns   there is nothing a batch of air buns won't cure   their batches hatch out of the oven fluffy and soft like chicks   after Dad's funeral over stacks of turkey buns and lots of wine the youngest brother   the baby   starts telling all the dirty jokes he knows and when our sides hurt from too much laughing he comes up with a few more   until we think we are going to die if he doesn't stop   and finally he confesses that his real reason for getting up first in the morning was not just to pee not just to get his thumb sucking fix before going to school   but because he liked to watch   to watch Mom's buns jiggle under her chiffon housecoat as she sliced bread for toast

found poem 3   fifty-three

two big stuck-together wax numbers planted right in the middle of the thick chocolate icing   fifty-three   "That's how old I am now!" i think   as i flip through a photo album   in this one Mom sits at the big brown table in the act of blowing out her candles daintily holding a cigarette as if she'd just started smoking the day before   and in the next picture there she is on the beach at Shaw's Point with a granddaughter and they're posing for the camera like old fashioned models   wearing the exact same navy blue bathing suit   "They look like sisters" people say "not like grandmother and granddaughter"   how young she looked is what everyone always said about Mom   and *comme elle est toujours si bien mise*   some even think she's a snob and we can't imagine she'll ever ever run out of energy but that last Christmas in the big house she burns the stuffing   and frets   nobody's done the damned walks she cries and she doesn't even change for the meal   she isn't hungry she says   and it's the first time Mom can't

diagnosis

the other funny thing about Mom is *quand a' s' décidait* that was it   like when our designer brother helped her build her dream home and she went to work two jobs to buy all the things she'd ever wanted   like a fire place and parquet flooring   and an area rug   and a full set of living room furniture love seat and all for her sunken living room   she planned for a cozy loft too and a well lit sewing room and lots and lots of storage space for once   and when she somehow knew it was time to move to the city that was it the whole place had to get cleaned and sorted   just like when we'd move *de la ferme au village*   just like the day she was diagnosed with Alzheimer's   three of us girls went to her that evening and she said i have it i have it i'll do my best   and i got quiet and the other two sisters got talkative and cracked open the vitamin encyclopedias and the nutrition magazines   and Mom said i have too many clothes so i sorted all day and do you want a cup of tea?   and we had cake that she and her husband had baked that day and nobody made a scene   and i knew Mom was resigned and she'd give up her high heels and her fancy dresses and it explained why she so suddenly got so impatient or mad for no reason at all and told everybody no one ever visited   because she forgot   and why she was so afraid to drive in the city and wouldn't even try   she'd say *j'ai ben trop peur de m' perdre*   the funny thing about Mom is she'd always been afraid of getting herself lost

getting it

at a symphony concert *ça m'surprend* Mom said that there are such young people in the orchestra   but she couldn't find the word orchestra and she'd often said things surprised her lately   and at intermission we had to go stand in a corner and no she didn't want a drink or a treat   and she would have been ready to go home then   even though she had gone to the hairdresser and had gotten all dressed up and looked really really classy   as if nothing at all nothing at all was wrong   and another time when we went to the free noon hour concert   before we knew and before i knew crowds spooked her   after i'd dragged her to the front where i like to sit and she'd squeezed my arm tighter and tighter as we milled our way through the crowd she got really bitchy   about dirty Kleenex tissues how she'd forgotten to put a fresh supply in her purse   again   and how she really hates the city   because it always costs you for parking *pis dans ces maudites places de fous* underground how do you find your damned way around anyways   and all she wanted to do after was go to the drugstore and once there she got flustered again and as i was driving home i got it   her nail polish fetish! they had moved the display and she couldn't find words to ask   cried *personne me comprend*

Halloween Day 1999

it has snowed this morning   the sky is the colour of the blessed Virgin Mary's robe   holy sad blue   i sit by my Mom's bedside as she falls in and out of sleep tosses and turns groans moans and whimpers   sits up ramrod straight like *Pépère Chu en train de tout perdr'* she utters as lucid as in her prime   knowing   nailing her truth on the head   and we know it too   we have to think of "placing" Mother in a "home"   this prospect is about as appealing as diving into a swimming pool drained of water for winter   i want to throw glasses against a concrete wall just to hear the shattering the sharp rippling ring of spilling shards in this stretched strung despair   sorrow in her costume of rags makes a grand entrance as my heart is already tuning in to a new beat to the slow speed of Alzheimer's drum   et *mes chaudes larmes se répandent* and i too am *bleu ciel*   the colour of Mary's robe

trouble

when we come to tell Mom she has to move she tells us to go home to mind our own business and that she and her husband yes she insists my husband and i damn it we're doing just fine together and again we should mind our own damned business he had phoned and said you can have your mother after the last episode where she was so constipated and had to have a homecare nurse in to dis-impact her after she just wouldn't drink the whole bottle of laxative after she'd tried and tried to make herself go and couldn't and had spread shit on the toilet seat trying to get it out of her with her fingers and she didn't want to be any trouble and she couldn't go and it hurt too much and when her husband phoned and said he wouldn't deal with her anymore wouldn't deal with shit when it gets to shit he's done we knew we were done too and had to do something the thing we dreaded vowed we would never do *jamais*

placing Mom

she pauses on the threshold says *ah ah c'est beau* and we know we have done our job well   even though we got the smallest room   made sure to include pink and lace and small plants for her one window   a pretty lamp and a big frame full of family pictures   and a cross with her last weaving   from *le dimanche des rameaux*   affixed to it   and just for today   i get to stay   for a lunch of soggy sandwiches and canned soup   and under-stand that i am to leave   right after lunch

                                              i take my leave

Thursdays with Mom

Thursday mornings i go spend time with Mom at the home but to her the home isn't "home"   there is nothing to do and she can't serve tea   it wouldn't be safe the staff explains   i'm not used to Mom doing nothing and neither is she and she's restless   and she becomes more herself when we can manage to go for a walk outside where she gets to point out the beauty of changing leaves and still revel in colour   and that there are ripe apples on some trees and she mimics stealing some   because most of her words are gone   and i play along with her   make fun   but she can't always be coaxed and it isn't always fun to be with her   so i take to going at night instead when i can put her to bed and tuck her in and remember that sleep has always been a balm to my Mom   she quietens and as i look into her young perfect eyes i know i'm the mother now

sewing basket

my Mom's Alzheimers rips seams breaks threads and frays the fabric of her crazy quilt life   steals her flesh   leaves a scant swatch of her dressed in an outfit of bare bones   jerking underneath her face like Mexican jumping beans sharp witty words and sudden snips of humour a few well placed cusses poke through her mouth   like needles on taut framed fabric   visitors clasp and button her to her past sometimes almost return a lost mother like a dome fastener   click into her love for babies and small children   thick like butterscotch on a sundae   restores briefly *le beau visage de notre mère* like a well darned sock and in her single bed at night she prays clasping her spring green rosary to her heart   this lulls her to early sleep   a too early sleep   and she starts to go to bed earlier and earlier   and the staff don't like that   because she gets up earlier   and earlier   and is hungry   and wants to be fed   and some of the residents like to sleep in   you know   and she's trouble

the boyfriend

my brother gets off the phone   it has been a long call and he's been smiling like the Cheshire Cat   and we know he's talking about Mom with our youngest sister who goes to the home once a week to paint the ladies' nails and do their hair and we can't imagine what is so funny about Mom   we haven't laughed for so long   he gets off the phone and says Mom has a boyfriend! and they are inseparable and the home wants to meet with family   soon   because they're sneaking into each other's beds in the middle of the night   and one fell off   and it's dangerous and what do we want to do?

double bed

and unanimously we decide to bring the lovers a double bed   there is flak from other residents and some staff shake their heads but we know this is her first and last fling and we want her to have it   so curious we all take turns to go size up this guy and mom has eyes only for him   and he for her   and they flirt all day   share each other's cookies and juice   and walk down the hallways holding hands   always sit real close   and he wants to know if one of us would have pre primers and primers to lend because he's noticed that she's lost her English and he's sure he can teach her how to read   then he gets really pensive and we're all sitting on the bed because there is no room left for chairs   declares you know my thing doesn't work anymore and he catches my stunned look and we burst out laughing and Mom laughs too   and he adds i'm glad because it gave me no end of trouble   no end of trouble   my whole life

c'est dur

and then we get the call   they can't handle her anymore   she's interfering with other residents   she grabs they say   our mother touches that's what she's always done   and she's lost all her words has only one harsh sound left "durr-durr-durr-durr"   and it's too hard annoying embarrassing   and she knows and doesn't know and tries to make fun   but it isn't catching and she has to be sedated to get into the car after we've edged her toward the door   and i unclasp her hand from the door frame push her right leg in fast

dépouillement

Mom doesn't know why the kerfuffle   why all of a sudden we're all there and bless her heart she is the one who soothes the boyfriend who's weeping   who knows where she is going   but she doesn't know and she tweaks his cheeks pulls at his chin makes him look at her   laugh   and they exchange that last look   and she doesn't know where she's going and no when we get there she doesn't want to stay   even though there are cats on that ward   *des maudits chats ça fait du poil partout*   and she walks in circles   back to the door of the lock up unit wants out wants out wants out   walks in crazy crazy circles

moving Mom

we got to "place" Mom twice to empty her rooms twice and each time there had to be less stuff the first time i'd snatched her rosary slipped it into my pocket a strong piece of her and a small pink bird that i had stuck in a plant i'd given her before i stopped giving things and the last time was the hardest because there she was dead on her bed and we were handed two black plastic garbage bags told the room has to be vacated by midnight and a sibling says No! one more brother is on his way and he has to see her so they gave us an extra hour and i threw everything pell-mell into those two bags including three mismatched men's slippers she had a thing for slippers in the end she'd hold them and rock them they were her babies Mom had always been fond of babies and dolls her first doll had been *une bûche de bois* with nails for arms and cotton remnants for clothes and she'd always say we were poor but we were happy because we were all together and it was hard for Mom when she had to start school along with her youngest sisters and two older brothers because someone from the school board said they had to go had even found accommodation so they were packed and moved to the edge of the village in a *grainerie* had to fend for themselves and the water in their wash basin was frozen over in the morning and evenings the girls were so scared of the coyotes' howls their brothers took to yodelling to cheer them up

panic

when the casket lid closes
when it is rolled down the aisle
toward the vestibule
when the church doors open
to the early setting sun
and her six pallbearer sons
haul her body into the hearse
when i can't stop the shaking
and it isn't from the cold
and it isn't quite over yet
there's one more detail
my sister and i think
about the burning –
but say nothing – till later
and still later   much later
i know what i needed then
not a roomful of relatives
and townsfolk   not small talk
not to hear for the hundredth time
how much i look like her
or to be asked which brother
comes after which   again
but   the open prairie
where i was conceived
where i could walk
and howl and howl

Greyhound Bus north

October is   space   a pause   between the in breath of autumn and the out breath of winter   to my left the landscape is lit up to my right it is dull   in between shine and dull dark and light life and death hang questions   from the bus window the prairie sky is a wide-open mouth feeding on fallow fields   What is this kinship I feel for the October landscape?   It is familiarity – the face of an old woman unadorned – as basic as soil   the one who was always underfoot   always making tea   it is the sound of *Mémère's* footsteps on the floorboards of the old farmhouse ⸴ setting one brown shoed foot squarely in front of the other   to keep going after *Pépère* died   it is the sh-sh-sh of dry grass shivers announcing the coming of winter   it is the cold wind over pioneer broken ground as it crosses the mind of the season shushing itself to sleep   it is the inevitable turning   the circle dance of things   grandma's apron-covered belly and her hands stirring the soup pot   it is eating and being eaten one season getting swallowed into the other   as the wheels of the bus turn   time arcs into space and *Mémère's* whole life's worth of hymn singing resounds loud and free proclaiming her long   long   longing   for home

Afterword

I couldn't wait to leave
mostly didn't want to be there
that first year I left   I
hardly made it to Thanksgiving
couldn't wait to go home
and once home
I couldn't wait
to leave again.
And   when I left for good
was sometimes seized
by a yearning for home
as visceral as the smell
of perking coffee
the buzz of shared cigarettes after supper
of a handful of soil

acknowledgements

I wish to thank the University of Alberta's Faculty of Extension for Woman's Writing Week and all the writers who came to teach, inspire and build community; the many participants and guests who have attended and performed at the Wind Eye Writing Seminars over the last eight years; the Stroll of Poets Society of Edmonton, especially the volunteers who make it possible for writers to perform at the Upper Crust Cafe's Poets Haven Series; and the anthology committee who design anthologies and chapbooks.

I am indebted to those who pushed the poetry along: to sheri-d wilson for inviting me to perform at the Calgary International Spoken Word Festival, for her enthusiasm, and for her dynamic and innovative teaching of the art of performance; to Eunice Scarfe of Saga Seminars for the prompt that sparked the manuscript; to Diane Buchanan and Myrna Garanis for their encouragement at the right moments; and to Dymphny Dionyk, Angela Kublik and all the volunteers for organizing the WGA 2007 Writing the Land Conference in Grande Prairie.

I also wish to thank Erinne Sevigny, editor of *Other Voices Journal of the Literary and Visual Arts* for her feedback on the *alzheimer's suite* and for the invitations to read; Barbara Dacks of *Legacy, Alberta's Magazine for New Heritage, Arts & Culture* for the conversations, the contests, and for her support of the arts; Sherrilyn Jahrig of Tangent Performance Group for inviting me and other members of our group to move the poetry to another level; Leslie Nicholson for nominating me Woman of Vision and Lesley MacDonald of Global Television for featuring my work with women and writing.

I am grateful to my gracious readers for the coaching and encouragement: Myrna Kostash, Robert Lalonde, Alice Major, Anne Gerard Marshall, Andy Michaelson, Jocelyne Verret, Jean Waters, and Marlyn Wall; to my sister Suzanne for the laughter and the tears; to the members of my extended family for their patience and their ears; and to my son Christian Durand for his deeply touching response to the stories.

This book could not have been written without the financial support of Norm. Thanks also for the computer.

I thank Lynn and Charlie for their hospitality during ten crucial days in their home.

I wish to thank *Mémère* Requier for her letters that became found poems 1 & 2.

While completing this manuscript, various pieces in progress appeared on CBC's *Wild Rose Country*, on the *Legacy Magazine* website, in the *Spires Poetry* poster and the *Stroll of Poets Anthology* (1999, 2007). A suite of poems appeared *in Other Voices Journal of the Literary and Visual Arts* Spring 2008, 20.2.

Many of these prose poems have been performed at launches, public readings and at festivals across Alberta.

Photo: Fred Katz

Pierrette Requier, a long time member of the Stroll of Poets Society of Edmonton, facilitates the Wind Eye Poetry Seminars. For the last ten years, she has been involved in spoken word performances as a student and as group facilitator. She has performed her poetry and monologues in both English and French in festivals and readings across Alberta, including Edmonton's 2007 *Word!* Gala, Calgary's *2008 Francophonétique,* and the Calgary International Spoken Word Festival and Edmonton's *Night of Artists* as a member of Tangent Lines. She has been a participant in a French writing and performance group *Les déesses de l'écriture* since 2005. Her poetry has appeared on CBC's Wild Rose Country, in *Legacy Alberta's Heritage Magazine, Other Voices Edmonton's Journal of the Literary and Visual Arts,* in *Writing the Land Anthology Alberta through its poets* and a number of other anthologies and websites.